LIFE CHANGING LESSONS FROM CELEBRITY BANKRUPTCIES

Turn Your Life Around By Studying How These Five Famous Debtors Coped With Their Own Money Troubles

By Ronald J. Drescher

I hope that reading this book helps you decide to contact our firm and schedule a free consult to talk about your problems and outline a solution. This consult, ***a value of over $195***, may help change your life, for all the reasons discussed in this book. If you want to skip forward and see why I believe this to be true, read the section called ***8 Pieces Of Life Changing Advice A Bankruptcy Lawyer Will Give You For Free*** that begins on page 26.

Please don't spend another hour today worrying about what's going to happen tomorrow. Call us at:

410-484-3088

We hope to see you soon.

Published by Ronald J. Drescher, Baltimore MD

Printed in the United States of America.

ISBN: ISBN- 13: 978-0692474129

ISBN- 10: 0692474129

Additional copies are available at special quantity discounts for bulk purchases for sales promotions, premiums, fundraising, and educational use.

For more information, please contact: Ronald Drescher, Drescher & Associates, 410-484-3088

Or visit our website, www.Drescherlaw.com

To find out what other clients have to say about their experience with our firm, visit DrescherReviews.com.
Contact the author directly at
bankruptcylessons@drescherlaw.com

Table Of Contents

Introduction

The law has a love/hate relationship with celebrities. Most people don't really care about that house broken into across town, the auto accident on the beltway or the family in foreclosure. But when the somebody walking up the courthouse steps has been nominated for an Oscar or featured on TMZ, the rules change.

Everyone wants to watch when a celebrity is in trouble. When Baltimore Ravens star running back Ray Rice was accused of domestic abuse the world paid close attention, especially after TMZ released the video of him punching his fiance in an elevator; in "real life" that elevator video would have been forgotten in police paperwork. OJ Simpson's 1994 trial was riveting daily TV on CNN and the troubles of Lindsay Lohan and Kim Kardashian will always draw a look on a supermarket tabloid.

So it is with bankruptcy as well. Kim Basinger, Burt Reynolds, Jerry Lewis, Cyndi Lauper, David Crosby, Tom Petty and many others have lived for years in the public eye.

Nevertheless, all of these “rich and famous” figures have had to file bankruptcy in their lives, and every bankrupt celebrity has to live by the same bankruptcy laws and follow the same bankruptcy procedures as the family struggling through a job loss, a business that's lost its biggest customer or a single mom who can’t collect on her child support. Watching these figures journey through their very public ordeals can help the rest of us make the right choices to better our lives by either emulating their skillful steps or avoiding their stumbles.

When clients come into my office for the first time they’re usually filled with fear, anxiety and dread. By the time they leave, most clients tell me that a weight has been lifted off their shoulders and they can sleep at night, often for the first time in years. Knowing I can help these men, women and families overcome their seeming impossible obstacles drives me every day. To help even more people, I wrote this book to guide readers through the life changing lessons hidden in the files of celebrity bankruptcies.

Lesson 1

Face The Facts To Change Your Life

The Bankruptcy of Kim Basinger

Kim Basinger made an oral agreement to appear in the Main Line Production *Boxing Helena.* Four weeks before production began she pulled out of the film, objecting to what she believed were scenes requiring gratuitous nudity. Main Line sued Basinger for breach of the oral agreement and won a jury verdict (later overturned on appeal) for $8.1 million. Basinger sought protection from Main Line by filing Chapter 11 bankruptcy.

Chapter 11 is a procedure that allows debtors to retain control over their assets while attempting to propose a plan of reorganization that will satisfy creditors. Built into the process is a need for the debtor to negotiate with at least some creditors who are not the debtor's relatives, employees or affiliates. Major creditors have more influence in Chapter 11 proceedings because a debtor needs to obtain the consents of creditors who vote to accept or reject the plan.

In Basinger's case, she faced a significant challenge from Main Line. Not only did she owe them over $8 million, they were hostile and demanding. In attempting to confirm her Chapter 11 repayment plan, Main Line wanted to have a say over what films Basinger made and other aspects of her future finances. Eventually, Basinger came to realize that making a deal with Main Line would allow her to keep her assets, but at an unacceptable price.

This is when the star faced the facts and came to see that her future was more important than her stuff. She converted her case from Chapter 11 to Chapter 7. This was a major concession and showed a great deal of courage and sense.

In Chapter 7 debtors may lose control of their assets because a trustee is appointed who legally is the owner of the assets for the benefit of creditors. During the time the trustee analyzes whether he can liquidate these assets and turn them into cash, the debtor almost always holds onto the assets. A debtor's furniture, car and even house usually remain in the debtor's custody and care during this process. It may take years for a trustee to decide whether an asset has value, and during this time it would be prohibitively expensive for the trustee to take possession of the asset and incur storage charges, although that does happen in rare occasions. Of course, if the debtor sells or destroys the property in his custody he risks losing his discharge or imprisonment, which is what happened to baseball great Lenny Dykstra as we will see below.

Receiving a discharge of the debt is a client's primary benefit for exposing his assets to sale by a Chapter 7 trustee. *Discharge is the legal benefit of being permanently relieved of having to pay a creditor. This is the main reason most people file for bankruptcy.* Presuming that the debtor has been truthful and transparent, in 60 days after the meeting with creditors and a trustee, the debtor will receive a discharge. In the absence of fraud or other misdeeds, creditors have no way to defeat that discharge. The debtor can keep his post-bankruptcy income and exemptions permitted by statute and emerge from bankruptcy debt free.

This was Basinger's decision. Understanding that she may lose real estate, valuable artwork and antiques, bank accounts and other assets, Basinger weighed the benefits of becoming clear of Main Line's right to veto her future career decisions against the anxiety of surrendering her assets. Basinger overcame this fear: Having fully disclosed her assets, debts, income and expenses, Basinger was able to receive her discharge and control her own destiny.

Exemptions: The Property You Can Keep In Bankruptcy

In the "real world", whether a trustee will be able to turn assets into cash for creditors depends in part upon *the exemptions* available in that state. Every state allows a debtor to retain some cash, assets, home furnishings and other property after receiving a discharge from bankruptcy. This retained property constitutes the debtor's exemptions because the assets are exempt from the right of a creditor or trustee to sell the assets and pay claims.

The exemptions differ from state to state. For example, in Maryland most debtors are allowed to keep approximately $12,000 of value in their assets, almost $23,000 of the equity in their home and all of their qualified retirement accounts. Other assets may also be available.

The trustees are well versed in the exemptions available to debtors. If a trustee evaluates the debtor's cash, tax refunds, jewelry, firearms and other belongings and determines that their aggregate value is less than the allowed exemptions, the trustee will quickly conclude that there will no benefit to going through the trouble of liquidation because creditors will get nothing. When that happens, the trustee files *a no distribution report*. Receiving this report is a great milestone for debtors.

On the other hand, many times a debtor owns property that is worth more than his allowed exemptions. In that event, the trustee will confront the debtor's attorney with a demand that the debtor turnover the surplus assets for the trustee to sell. A key strategy for the debtor will be to negotiate with the trustee, paying a reasonable amount to allow the debtor to keep that surplus property. This happens most of the time when the value of the assets does not significantly exceed the allowed exemptions because *the debtor is the trustee's best buyer*. By selling the surplus back to the debtor the trustee doesn't need to expend costs to store, appraise, auction or deliver the property, which remains in the debtor's possession.

Kim Basinger's life changed when she faced the facts, converted her case to Chapter 7 and her trustee opened an estate. Basinger was free from Main Line and went on to win an Oscar for her role in LA Confidential. None of that may have happened had she stayed in Chapter 11.

Frequently Asked Question:
Can an Individual File for Chapter 11?

If you can't quality for Chapter 7 or 13, you may still get bankruptcy relief under Chapter 11. Why would you need to do that?

If your income is too high and you don't have sufficient deductions, you're probably going to be forced out of Chapter 7 by *the means test*. This is a test that determines whether a debtor who owes primarily consumer debts has sufficient means to repay some of their debt. The focus of the bankruptcy court is on the debtor's household income. If this income is over the median income of that debtor's state, there is a risk that the debtor won't qualify to discharge all of their debts in Chapter 7. (For example, as of 2015 the median income in Maryland for an individual debtor is just under $60,000, and for a family of four is approximately $107,000. Maryland, however, is one of the highest median income states). If the debtor doesn't qualify for a complete discharge in Chapter 7, the next question is, can the debtor file for Chapter 13?

Chapter 13 is a procedure for debtors to obtain a discharge over a period of three to five years by making monthly payments to a Chapter 13 trustee. This trustee, unlike a Chapter 7 trustee, doesn't have the power to sell your assets; a Chapter 13 trustee is really an administrator who reviews proposed payment plans and, once approved, collects the debtor's payments and pays out to creditors. After all the payments are made, the debtor receives the same discharge he would have received immediately in Chpater 7.

Chapter 13, however, is not available to everyone. If a debtor owes too much of either secured debt (like a home mortgage or a car payment) or unsecured debt (like credit cards, taxes and student loans), then the debtor won't qualify for Chapter 13. These debt limits fluctuate from year to year based on the cost of living, but they are set by statute and they are rigidly enforced (as of 2015, for unsecured debt, the limit is about $385,000; for secured debt, about $1,100,000).

If you don't qualify under the debt limits for Chapter 13, and your gross income is too high for Chapter 7, you won't necessarily be deprived of relief under the bankruptcy laws, because you might qualify for Chapter 11. Chapter 11 is a procedure for businesses, but also for high-income individuals with a fairly sophisticated financial situation who want or need to file their own plan of reorganization to reorder their financial affairs. Under Chapter 11, the debtor proposes their own plan, and creditors have a right to vote to accept or reject the proposal. If the plan succeeds, the treatment the debtor promises under the *plan of reorganization* substitutes the debts the debtor owed when they filed bankruptcy. Chapter 11 is a much more flexible process than Chapter 13.

Lesson Learned: Jackie's Story

Jackie changed her life after filing Chapter 7 bankruptcy. She did everything she could to avoid filing, trying to short sell her home to keep it out of foreclosure. Unfortunately, she had to face the facts and realize that she couldn't pay off the promissory note the lender required as part of the short sale. Jackie retained me to represent her in bankruptcy, and this is what she had to say when it was all over:

This is an easy recommendation.

Ron Drescher is one of the finest bankruptcy attorneys you will ever find. The entire time, through this complex process, Mr. Drescher was amazing. Filing bankruptcy was such a difficult decision but he anticipated every aspect of the process expertly. I was so unsure of filing - even though there really was no other choice for me. However, with his guidance and experience he made me feel completely comfortable and informed. I have talked with many people who have gone through bankruptcy with other attorneys - and they did not get the same high level of professionalism that Mr. Drescher consistently demonstrated. His depth of knowledge about bankruptcy and the court system was extensive and comforting. He was completely available by any form of communication - email, text, phone, etc. I had dreaded the prospect of bankruptcy, but was forced into it after an ugly short sale gone bad. Going to Ron Drescher for advice was the best financial decision that I have ever made. He was able to help me re-establish my fiscal life and gain emotional piece of mind. I can't thank him enough.

My advice - DON'T HESITATE, call him for advice today! He was so easy and comfortable to talk to. His knowledge is outstanding. Thanks!

Lesson 2

Be Ready For The Public To See You Change Your Life

The Bankruptcy of Casey Anthony

Every bankruptcy case involves at least one public appearance for the debtor: the meeting of creditors. Whether this event is called the "meeting of creditors," the "meeting with the trustee" or the "341 meeting" (based on the section of the Bankruptcy Code that is the legal basis for the meeting) certain aspects are always true:

- The debtor will testify under oath about their income, expenses, assets and liabilities;
- The meeting takes place towards the beginning of the case, usually 30-40 days after filing;
- The meeting will be set in a public place.

Few meetings of creditors were ever more highly anticipated than Casey Anthony's. Even though she was ultimately acquitted of murdering her 2 year old daughter Kaylee, the publicity surrounding her murder trial was so negative that she became almost universally reviled. After stepping out of her

Florida jail in July, 2011, Casey Anthony went into hiding. Public interest in her doings and whereabouts remained intense, but few legitimate reports emerged about her. The world was shocked when only 18 months later Anthony filed bankruptcy in Tampa.

Anthony's bankruptcy schedules became the source of feverish interest on the celebrity web. Bloggers dissected her assets and liabilities, speculating on how Anthony would handle the media spotlight expected for her meeting of creditors.

The court made special arrangements for the event, changing the normal setting to a large auditorium that could accommodate the anticipated swarm of media. When Anthony emerged from a black SUV surrounded by her lawyers she was engulfed by reporters and photographers. US Marshals and Homeland Security agents escorted her to the meeting room, where she was met by more reporters, the trustee and an attorney for one creditor.

From all accounts, Casey Anthony was well dressed and well prepared. She wore a white short-sleeve top, a black skirt and black heels. She consulted frequently with her attorneys and when she spoke, it was in a calm, matter-of-fact voice, and she mostly answered "yes sir" or "no sir" to the trustee's questions.

Casey Anthony was obviously ready for her first public appearance since the shocking verdict in her sensational trial. Her lawyers had helped her prepare and there were no surprises.

Obviously, when a bankrupt celebrity meets with creditors and the trustee there is an opportunity for the press and the public to scrutinize that celebrity in this potentially embarrassing role. Understanding this, celebrities come prepared for the event. Such preparation usually involves anticipating the trustee's questions, but more importantly, includes being thoroughly familiar with the bankruptcy papers they filed under oath.

Facing a creditors' meeting? Here is a good list of 7 steps to prepare for that event:

1. Bring your photo I.D. and Social Security card. Bankruptcy trustees need to be able to establish that you are who you say you are in your bankruptcy papers. To do this they need

an original document containing your complete Social Security number. Bringing your Social Security card is easiest, but your W2 or annual Social Security earnings statement will work too. Bear in mind you need the complete Social Security number: Your tax return will not qualify because it is not a government-issued document. The trustee will likely postpone your meeting of creditors if you don't have proper documentation. That will make you, your attorney, and the trustee very unhappy.

2. Carefully review your bankruptcy papers a day or two before the meeting. The trustee may ask if there are any corrections to your schedules, so if you answer no, be sure that you are giving an informed answer. Don't expect to plead lack of knowledge if it turns out there is a material omission or mistake in these papers and you didn't catch it in time to tell the trustee. This may be your last meaningful chance to make sure that you have provided a complete disclosure of your assets, debts, income, and expenses.

3. Confirm the meeting's date, time and place with your lawyer. Make sure that your lawyer or another attorney will be there with you. If not, reschedule. This is an important day and nothing should be left to chance.

4. Know where you're going. This may be the only trip you ever make to a federal building. You are going to be stressed enough anticipating the questions of the trustee without having the additional stress of getting lost as you make your way to a place you've never been before.

5. Leave time to get through security. Many meetings of creditors are held in federal courthouses, all of which now have security scanning to rival an international airport. You should add another ten minutes of your travel time to get through. In addition, you should call ahead to make sure that your cell phone, iPad, laptop, or any other electronic device is permitted inside the building. You would hate to have to throw that valuable item into the bushes outside the courthouse only to find it gone when you return.

6. Ignore the gallery. In a typical no-asset Chapter 7 case the norm is that no creditors will attend and the trustee will be done with you in ten minutes. The meeting will, however, be held in a public place so other debtors, their attorneys and creditors are likely to be in attendance. Ignore them and relax; for them your case is just something they have to sit through until their case is called.

7. If a creditor does appear, answer their questions fully and truthfully and helpfully. Creditors are usually not looking to hurt you, only to get paid. Let them ask their questions. Creditors are only allowed to ask questions about your financial condition. The trustee or your lawyer will stop the questioning if they go too far afield.

Frequently Asked Question:
Why Is The Trustee So Interested In My Bankruptcy Case?

The answer to this question becomes clear when you understand that a Chapter 7 trustee is a private attorney appointed to a panel by the Department of Justice. Trustees are paid only

$65.00 per case according to statute and this is the total payment for approximately 95 percent of their cases. By looking closely at bankruptcy schedule details, in about 5 percent of their cases, trustees identify assets to use for paying creditors.

When a trustee succeeds in finding assets to pay creditors, they get paid more than the $65.00 minimum fee. At that point, they can then hire their own law firm and be paid $300.00 to $500.00 an hour. In addition to the hourly billing rate, the trustee will also receive a percentage of the amount paid to creditors. Since trustees in Chapter 7 cases really only get paid after they collect assets, they take a very close look at every case.

Lesson Learned: Heather's Story

Heather had a highly complex problem involving her income and child support received, and the Chapter 13 trustee objected to her plan. In many Chapter 13 cases plan disputes can be resolved by discussions with the trustee, but in her case Heather needed to go to court and tell her story to the bankruptcy judge. Here's what happened, in her own words:

Even on Christmas Eve

Mr Drescher met with me first on Christmas Eve. He explained everything that would happen and even argued before a judge rather than give up and give in. He was well prepared and we prevailed saving me over 500+ a month. Couldn't be happier. That was a very stressful time and he helped lessen a lot of that.

Lesson 3

Changing Your Life Is More Important Than What Other People Think

The Bankruptcy of Walt Disney

His name may be iconic today, but early in his career, Walt Disney was just a struggling filmmaker in Kansas City with too many bills. In 1922 he started his first film company named Laugh-O-Gram. Disney even signed a deal with a New York company to distribute the films he was producing, but the distributor stole from him. Without the distributor's cash, Disney couldn't cover his overhead, and his studio went bankrupt in 1923.

He then left Kansas City for Hollywood, and after a series of increasingly successful creations, Disney debuted a new character named Mickey Mouse in 1928. After that, his life changed forever.

Walt Disney could have stayed behind in Kansas City working on a farm had he never overcome his feelings of failure and shame to file his bankruptcy case. In my video *Is There a*

Stigma to Filing for Bankruptcy? I explored the question of why so many people hold themselves back from making the decision to take the steps needed to move forward with their lives. Curiously, although they are in the public eye, celebrities will often brave the shame and scorn of a judgmental world to make the right decision for themselves and their families.

The perceived stigma of public shaming that debtors fear from bankruptcy can be so great that clients will make ruinous decisions about their own financial health. The worst decision? Invading a retirement account to pay dischargeable debts.

I wrote a blog item called 8 Pieces Of Life Changing Advice A Bankruptcy Lawyer Will Give You For Free. The blog was intended as a call to action for distressed debtors to seek legal advice, usually given for free, from a bankruptcy lawyer. One of the most important points I emphasized was that "Without paying a dime a client will learn that ... they should not invade their IRA or 401(k)". When I wrote this I insisted that this is free advice that, if taken, may change the course of lives, families ***and even generations***.

Was this just a puff piece? I didn't think so then and I don't think so now, especially with the explosive growth in the equities markets since that blog's publication in July, 2012. The real truth is that if a family has $100,000 in a protected retirement account when the parents are, say, 45 years old, that money can grow tax free until withdrawals become forced at the age of 70. So if the money grows at 4%, the value in 25 years will be $266,583.63. If the money grows at 7% the value will be $542,743.26. (Source? Future Value Calculator, http://www.investopedia.com/calculator/fvcal.aspx).

Let's get back to the 45 year old parents with $100,000 in an IRA. They may have income interruption, bills to pay, a struggling business. Do they invade the IRA or consider bankruptcy? If they invade the IRA and spend the $100,000, they will incur a 10% penalty (usually withheld upon an early withdrawal) and then the rest of the $100,000 goes immediately into taxable income, probably forcing the client into a higher tax bracket. If the taxes aren't paid then and there, the unpaid tax liability (and the interest on the taxes) will become nondischargeable in bankruptcy, compelling the client into an installment plan with the IRS over several years.

When this happens the balance sheet of the family will become very ugly.

Can they recover in 25 years? Perhaps. ***If not, then the family will be left not only without the $542,000 they may have had, but also without the extra money the IRS will grab in the years to come after the decision was made to invade the retirement account***. This money could have been added to the IRA or 401(k) and further increased the family's net worth, significantly affecting the family for a very long time.

Walt Disney knew that he had to make the hard choice to file bankruptcy and leave Kansas City behind. He wasn't held back by the fears and anxieties of what his friends, family or neighbors might think. He knew he had a great future ahead and that changing his life was more important than what anyone else might think.

Frequently Asked Question:

I Have A Little Extra Cash, Should I Make An IRA Contribution Before I File Bankruptcy?

The answer to this question is not very clear, because there are many factors that go into whether or not making a contribution to your IRA on the eve of your bankruptcy case is a transaction that would be considered to have been done in good faith. Typically you are allowed to perform what's called **pre-bankruptcy planning** before filing your bankruptcy case. This involves arranging your affairs so that you pay as little as possible to the trustee after you file bankruptcy. The concern when you make an IRA contribution is that you're taking money that would have been available to pay creditors and putting it into a retirement account that is almost universally considered to be an exempt asset that the trustee and creditors can't reach.

Nevertheless, this kind of planning is usually permitted by the bankruptcy court. However, if there's a perception that a debtor has been too aggressive in spending their cash or rearranging their assets before they file bankruptcy, the court could find that the filing was in bad faith, or the exemption is denied, or in the worst case scenario, that the discharge will be denied because you transferred assets within a year before the bankruptcy, with an intent to hinder, defeat or delay your creditors. If that happens, it will likely be a problem without a solution. Proper pre-bankruptcy planning is a subtle and sensitive process, and if it's not handled property the results could be disastrous.

Lesson Learned: Earl's Story

Earl came to me with nearly $500,000 in past due taxes. I was not his first consult. Every other lawyer he talked to advised that back taxes are not dischargeable in bankruptcy. Fortunately for Earl, he did not stop his search for the correct advice. He found our firm, and here's his experience, in his own words:

Honest, upfront and no games

I hired Ron for a tricky bankruptcy with close to a half a million dollars in tax liens. After countless attorneys telling me it could not be done, I now have in my possession not only a clean discharge (my credit reports show zero past due accounts) but I also have documentation from both the state and the IRS that all liens have been released and they consider them to be discharged. My advice: Hire Ron, give him what he needs, and go back to living your life. He knows what he is doing.

Earl's story has an even happier ending. He recently sent me this email:

All 3 scores mid 7s. Not one lien shows on any bureau. 23 months out of BK and just got approved. Not qualified, but flat out thru underwriting approved for a house. They say to never forget those who helped you along the way, so thanks again for your professionalism and honesty in an occupation where those two words are seldom associated with one another.

Earl was able to change his life by following his own instincts and searching for the right answer to his problems.

Lesson 4

Change Your Life By Showing Off Your Best Self

The Bankruptcy of Lenny Dykstra

The heart and soul of the bankruptcy fresh start is complete and accurate disclosure of your assets, debts, income and expenses. When a person files bankruptcy he or she becomes the caretaker of their assets while the trustee decides what action to take. The trustee's first and best source of information is the debtor's own schedules, prepared and filed under penalty of perjury.

Even though the schedules do contain that threat of punishment if the debtor lies, perjury is difficult to prove and seldom prosecuted. In bankruptcy, however, serious fraud can bring serious consequences, as discovered in the worst way possible by baseball great Lenny Dykstra.

What did Dykstra do? Prosecutors say he hid, sold or destroyed more than $400,000 worth of items without permission of the bankruptcy trustee. Court documents show Dykstra said he put an oven, sconces and chandeliers into a storage unit, but prosecutors said he actually sold the items for $8,500. He also hid baseball gloves, balls, bats and other memorabilia from the bankruptcy court and creditors and sold them later for about $15,000. So, what did prosecutors prove? After a career of World Series glory and millions of dollars, Dykstra threw it all away for just over twenty thousand dollars, spending a year in federal prison and losing his right to a bankruptcy discharge.

Many debtors hide relatively minor assets from the trustee not so much out of greed, but more out of fear: fear of impoverishment, fear of losing their former elevated sense of themselves, fear of losing control. What they find is that the cost of this fear is usually far greater than the value of the hidden assets.

Prosecution for bankruptcy fraud is rare, but losing a bankruptcy discharge is not. Complete disclosure of assets, debts, income and expenses is the cornerstone of the bankruptcy world. As Lenny Dykstra has sadly learned, the meager profits of a fraudulent bankruptcy case rarely equal the complete relief enjoyed by the honest debtor.

Frequently Asked Question:

Do I Qualify For Bankruptcy If I'm Current On My Bills But Going To Have A Problem Next Month?

The short answer is "Probably yes" and this is true wherever you live. When you realize that paying bills the next month may not be doable, it is only natural to ask yourself if you qualify for bankruptcy. You should consider filing for bankruptcy when facing an inability to pay personal bills, even when you're able to pay your current bills. Bankruptcy laws don't take into consideration whether you are current or not current in paying your personal bills. A bankruptcy court:

- Considers what your income and expenses are to decide whether you qualify to file for Chapter 7.
- Checks whether you've listed all assets and all creditors.
- Sends a notice to creditors about your bankruptcy filing.

If nobody objects to your bankruptcy case, the court will enter your bankruptcy discharge. This discharge will usually cover credit card bills, medical bills, judgments arising from evictions, foreclosures, repossessed cars and other normal debts. The discharge will usually not cover student loans, income taxes for taxes due within the three years before bankruptcy, obligations arising from a divorce or criminal fines, such as traffic and parking tickets.

Lesson Learned: John's Story

John had made a bad business mistake, bringing in a junior partner who stole his money and almost ruined his good name. He needed to file Chapter 11 bankruptcy to complete the messy litigation with his partner and put his business back on a sound footing. The lawsuit continued in bankruptcy, but John was prepared to present himself in the best possible light, and today his business is thriving. Here's what he had to say:

Honest and experienced

Ron Drescher is and has been during 3 years of very adversarial proceedings ...the best attorney I have known in thirty-five years in business. He is prepared and thorough and honest. His billings are fair and accurate. He does not spend your time or money on lavish office space, keeps his rates reasonable and yet has years of experience. I could not have chosen a better firm.

Lesson 5

Change your life!

The Bankruptcy of Tom Petty

Bankruptcy is a life-changing event. When I meet most of my clients their finances are in chaos, their income uncertain and, in many cases, their self esteem at an all time low. I created my video playlist *Why Filing Bankruptcy May Be The Best Thing You Ever Do* (https://www.youtube.com/playlist?list=PLC057E167DC899667) so that viewers facing money problems could begin to understand that filing bankruptcy can be a catalyst for great change. That's what happened to Tom Petty when he filed bankruptcy.

At the time of Tom Petty's 1979 bankruptcy filing, he was still struggling even though he had already released two hit albums: Tom Petty and The Heartbreakers and You're Gonna Get It! Petty refused to allow his next album to be released, even going so far as to bear the cost of recording it personally, leaving him

$500,000 in debt. Petty's bankruptcy was an attempt to reject an unfavorable contract that Petty felt he had signed under duress.

One of the extraordinary powers of bankruptcy is the ability to get out from under burdensome contracts as part of a debtor's fresh start. This power is known as "rejecting an executory contract" (an executory contract is simply an agreement where there remains performance due on both sides). Petty was testing the waters in an uncertain area of the bankruptcy law at the time, because his record deal was a personal services contract. Since the Petty case, many courts have held that if these contracts contain exclusive rights for the debtor's services then the debtor will be held to those obligations even if they file for bankruptcy. A perfect example of how this works is in the recording industry.

Frequently, a fledgling recording artist signs an exclusive deal to deliver albums to a record company over a certain period of time: say three albums in three years. After two years and two albums, the artist may come to realize that he made a bad deal and want to terminate the agreement so he can make more money from his third album. To get out of that deal he can file for bankruptcy.

When this happens, the recording company has two remedies: a right to sue the artist for breach of contract to recover profits the record company should have made from releasing the third album, and a right to exclude the artist from recording a third album for any other company during the rest of the time that the contract is due to run. To enforce this right, the record company could ask a court to issue an injunction against the artist signing with another label (or creating his own label).

Under the bankruptcy law of rejecting contracts, the courts have held that while a bankrupt debtor could discharge a party's right to seek damages for the money losses after a breach or a rejection of the contract, that party could still obtain the injunction to prevent the bankrupt from offering his services to another bidder.

This was the difficult choice facing Tom Petty. He knew that he could create another album that would be enormously successful, but he wanted to capture more of the profits from that album than he would receive under his present contract with his record company, MCA. Petty's tradeoff was that he would file bankruptcy, discharge MCA's right to sue him for money damages, but at the same time have to sit out the last year of the contract. Petty was willing to make this hard choice because he knew that his long term financial future would benefit. Petty pulled the trigger on his bankruptcy and got ready for the long and difficult fight with his record company.

Ultimately, MCA agreed to release Petty from his existing contract but immediately re-signed him to a $3 million contract with a new subsidiary label created especially for this purpose. The album that Petty had held back, Damn The Torpedoes (featuring the singles "Refugee" and "Don't Do Me Like That"), would go on to be certified Double Platinum and make Tom Petty and The Heartbreakers into true superstars.

Tom Petty's life changed when he got out from under his burdensome contract, accepted the costs of his decision, and made a fresh start with his record company. None of this may have ever happened if he hadn't filed for bankruptcy.

Frequently Asked Question:

If I decide to file bankruptcy, will the creditors stop calling me?

Creditors must stop calling you once you actually file your bankruptcy case. That is the only time they are legally required to cease efforts to collect from you.

However, my office has a special program called the Pre-Bankruptcy Planning Program. In the Pre-Bankruptcy Planning Program my firm is retained to engage in specific planning before you file your case. This planning generally requires that we delay filing the bankruptcy case in order to achieve an important objective, such as: spending down surplus assets to qualify for exemptions; allowing the deadline to pass to discharge certain tax debts; qualifying to file your case in a preferred jurisdiction; or for many other purposes.

During this pre-bankruptcy period, clients refer their creditors to us, and we obtain temporary relief by explaining that we have been retained for bankruptcy. Creditors must stop calling at this point and almost always suspend their collection efforts.

Lesson Learned: Matt's Story

Matt felt as if his life was crumbling as he struggled through a painful divorce. He had spent what seemed like a fortune renovating a property he and his wife were going to live in as their dream home. When he came to see me there seemed no way out for him. Here's his story, in his own words:

A Thoughtful and Helpful Guide Through a Difficult Process

My case was not simple. I came to Ron when I had come to a point of no return. I did not know how to handle the debt load I was carrying from a divorce and to be honest - I felt like I had nowhere else to go. I searched online, researching out respected lawyers in the field, but I was confused. There was so much information, but very little was made easy and clear. I came across Ron's reviews and I decided to talk to him. I was lucky. Upon sitting down with him for an hour I knew I had met the right person to help me. He listened to me, respecting my situation and the history that brought me to his door. He was not judgmental, but instead was so very open and forthright about the process and what it means, both emotionally, but also realistically relative to its impact on life.

I originally thought a Chapter 13 was in my future, but after working with Ron it became a Chapter 7. Getting materials together was time consuming and nerve wracking. The more detail you provide the easier it is for later in the process. Ron has a mechanism in place that really makes the overall steps you need to take rather easy to complete, but also understand. He was always more than willing to work with me through the steps, quick to answer my calls or respond to an email, even during holidays and late at night. His staff was a few minutes away at all times. More than once I literally just dropped into his office, unannounced, and stole a few minutes of his time, or his staff's time, to get clarification on a concern. It is rare for an office to be that open for their clients. I was always greatly appreciative of their hard work, and true openness and caring they had for the process and me.

Once the case started Ron served as a guide. There were challenges, as I mentioned earlier, it was not cut and dry, but he helped me through it, keeping me sane when I thought I could not handle anymore. He was a voice of reason and a mentor all at once. The case was completed in a shorter timeframe than I expected, and crazy as it sounds, it all came together as planned. The unusualness of my case at times made me think it would not, and I was ok with that, as we had done the best we could, being honest and forthright, but at the end of the day, it ended as Ron predicted. Not a single step came before us that he did not understand and that he was not ready to address, ensuring that the process kept moving forward.

I highly recommend working with Ron and his team. They always treated me fairly and with respect. I believe they are in the business of changing people's lives. I know they changed mine.

Conclusion

If you're reading this book, you may be wondering whether bankruptcy will change your life. If you are struggling with your debt, afraid of losing your home or worried about your business, we may have a solution for you. Please feel free to visit my website, watch my YouTube videos or call me. You may be only one phone call away from changing your own life.

Ronald J. Drescher
Drescher & Associates, P.A
4 Reservoir Circle, Suite 107
Baltimore, MD 21208
(410) 484-3088
Fax (410) 484-8120

Delaware Office - 1 Commerce Center
1201 North Orange Street, Suite 722
Wilmington, Delaware 19801
Rondrescher@Drescherlaw.com

http://www.Drescherlaw.com
MDBankruptcyLawyer – YouTube

Printed in Dunstable, United Kingdom

91218879R00030